D1383990

Jan. 24, 1950

Joann Horton

As a Man Thinketh
and
Out from the Heart

BY

JAMES ALLEN

PHILADELPHIA
DAVID McKAY COMPANY
WASHINGTON SQUARE

CONTENTS

AS A MAN THINKETH

OUT FROM THE HEART

iv   Contents

As a Man Thinketh

FOREWORD

THIS little volume (the result of meditation and experience) is not intended as an exhaustive treatise on the much-written-upon subject of the power of thought. It is suggestive rather than explanatory, its object being to stimulate men and women to the discovery and perception of the truth that—

" They themselves are makers of themselves "

by virtue of the thoughts which they choose and encourage; that mind is the master-weaver, both of the inner garment of character and the outer garment of circumstance, and that, as they may have hitherto woven in ignorance and pain they may now weave in enlightenment and happiness.

JAMES ALLEN

THOUGHT AND CHARACTER

THE aphorism, "As a man thinketh in his heart so is he," not only embraces the whole of a man's being, but is so comprehensive as to reach out to every condition and circumstance of his life. A man is literally *what he thinks,* his character being the complete sum of all his thoughts.

As the plant springs from, and could not be without, the seed, so every act of a man springs from the hidden seeds of thought, and could not have appeared without them. This applies equally to those acts called " spon-

taneous" and "unpremeditated" as to
those which are deliberately executed.

Act is the blossom of thought, and
joy and suffering are its fruits; thus
does a man garner in the sweet and
bitter fruitage of his own husbandry.

"Thought in the mind hath made us. What
          we are
  By thought was wrought and built. If a
          man's mind
  Hath evil thoughts, pain comes on him
          as comes
  The wheel the ox behind. . . .
                         . . . If one endure
  In purity of thought, joy follows him
  As his own shadow—sure."

Man is a growth by law, and not a
creation by artifice, and cause and
effect are as absolute and undeviating
in the hidden realm of thought as in
the world of visible and material
things. A noble and God-like character is not a thing of favour or

chance, but is the natural result of continued effort in right thinking, the effect of long-cherished association with God-like thoughts. An ignoble and bestial character, by the same process, is the result of the continued harbouring of grovelling thoughts.

Man is made or unmade by himself; in the armoury of thought he forges the weapons by which he destroys himself; he also fashions the tools with which he builds for himself heavenly mansions of joy and strength and peace. By the right choice and true application of thought, man ascends to the Divine Perfection; by the abuse and wrong application of thought, he descends below the level of the beast. Between these two extremes are all the grades of character, and man is their maker and master.

Of all the beautiful truths pertaining to the soul which have been restored and brought to light in this age, none is more gladdening or fruitful of divine promise and confidence than this—that man is the master of thought, the moulder of character, and the maker and shaper of condition, environment, and destiny.

As a being of Power, Intelligence, and Love, and the lord of his own thoughts, man holds the key to every situation, and contains within himself that transforming and regenerative agency by which he may make himself what he wills.

Man is always the master, even in his weakest and most abandoned state; but in his weakness and degradation he is the foolish master who misgoverns his "household." When he begins to reflect upon his condition, and to search diligently for the Law upon which his being is established, he then becomes the wise master, directing his energies with intelligence, and fashioning his thoughts to fruitful issues. Such is the *conscious* master, and man can only thus become by discovering *within himself* the laws of thought; which discovery is totally a matter of application, self-analysis, and experience.

Only by much searching and mining are gold and diamonds obtained, and man can find every truth connected with his being, if he will dig deep into the mine of his soul; and that he is the maker of his character, the moulder of his life, and the builder of his destiny, he may unerringly prove, if he will watch, control, and alter his

thoughts, tracing their effects upon
himself, upon others, and upon his
life and circumstances, linking cause
and effect by patient practice and
investigation, and utilising his every
experience, even to the most trivial,
everyday occurrence, as a means of
obtaining that knowledge of himself
which is Understanding, Wisdom,
Power. In this direction, as in no
other, is the law absolute that " He
that seeketh findeth; and to him that
knocketh it shall be opened "; for only
by patience, practice, and ceaseless
importunity can a man enter the
Door of the Temple of Knowledge.

EFFECT OF THOUGHT ON
CIRCUMSTANCES

A MAN'S mind may be likened to a garden, which may be intelligently cultivated or allowed to run wild; but whether cultivated or neglected, it must, and will, *bring forth*. If no useful seeds are *put* into it, then an abundance of useless weed-seeds will *fall* therein, and will continue to produce their kind.

Just as a gardener cultivates his plot, keeping it free from weeds, and growing the flowers and fruits which he requires, so may a man tend the garden of his mind, weeding out all the wrong, useless, and impure thoughts, and cultivating toward perfection the flowers and fruits of right, useful, and pure thoughts. By pursuing this process, a man sooner or later discovers that he is the master-gardener of his soul, the director of his life. He also reveals, within himself, the laws of thought, and understands, with ever-increasing accuracy, how the thought-forces and mind-elements operate in the shaping of his character, circumstances, and destiny.

Thought and character are one, and as character can only manifest and discover itself through environment and circumstance, the outer conditions of a person's life will always be found to be harmoniously related to his inner state. This does not mean that a man's circumstances at any given time are an indication of his *entire* character, but that those circumstances are so intimately connected with some vital thought-element within himself that, for the time being, they are indispensable to his development.

Every man is where he is by the law of his being; the thoughts which he has built into his character have brought him there, and in the arrangement of his life there is no element of chance, but all is the result of a law which cannot err. This is just as true of those who feel "out of harmony" with their surroundings as of those who are contented with them.

As a progressive and evolving being, man is where he is that he may learn that he may grow; and as he learns the spiritual lesson which any circumstance contains for him, it passes away and gives place to other circumstances.

Man is buffeted by circumstances so long as he believes himself to be the creature of outside conditions, but when he realises that he is a creative power, and that he may command the hidden soil and seeds of his being out of which circumstances grow, he then becomes the rightful master of himself.

That circumstances *grow* out of thought every man knows who has for any length of time practised self-control and self-purification, for he will have noticed that the alteration in his circumstances has been in exact ratio with his altered mental condition. So true is this that when a man earnestly applies himself to remedy the defects in his character, and makes swift and marked progress, he passes rapidly through a succession of vicissitudes.

The soul attracts that which it secretly harbours; that which it loves, and also that which it fears; it reaches the height of its cherished aspirations; it falls to the level of its unchastened desires,—and circumstances are the means by which the soul receives its own.

Every thought-seed sown or allowed to fall into the mind, and to take root there, produces its own, blossoming sooner or later into act, and bearing its own fruitage of opportunity and circumstance. Good thoughts bear good fruit, bad thoughts bad fruit.

The outer world of circumstance shapes itself to the inner world of

thought, and both pleasant and un-
pleasant external conditions are fac-
tors which make for the ultimate good
of the individual. As the reaper of
his own harvest, man learns both by
suffering and bliss.

Following the inmost desires, aspirations, thoughts, by which he allows
himself to be dominated (pursuing
the will-o'-the-wisps of impure imaginings or steadfastly walking the high-
way of strong and high endeavour), a
man at last arrives at their fruition
and fulfilment in the outer conditions
of his life. The laws of growth and
adjustment everywhere obtain.

A man does not come to the pot-
house or the gaol by the tyranny of
fate or circumstance, but by the pathway of grovelling thoughts and base
desires. Nor does a pure-minded man

fall suddenly into crime by stress of any mere external force; the criminal thought had long been secretly fostered in the heart, and the hour of opportunity revealed its gathered power. Circumstance does not make the man; it reveals him to himself. No such conditions can exist as descending into vice and its attendant sufferings apart from vicious inclinations, or ascending into virtue and its pure happiness without the continued cultivation of virtuous aspirations; and man, therefore, as the lord and master of thought, is the maker of himself, the shaper and author of environment. Even at birth the soul comes to its own, and through every step of its earthly pilgrimage it attracts those combinations of conditions which reveal itself, which are

the reflections of its own purity and
impurity, its strength and weakness.

Men do not attract that which they
want, but that which they *are.* Their
whims, fancies, and ambitions are
thwarted at every step, but their inmost thoughts and desires are fed
with their own food, be it foul or
clean. The " divinity that shapes our
ends " is in ourselves; it is our very
self. Man is manacled only by himself; thought and action are the
gaolers of Fate—they imprison, being
base; they are also the angels of
Freedom—they liberate, being noble.
Not what he wishes and prays for
does a man get, but what he justly
earns. His wishes and prayers are only
gratified and answered when they harmonise with his thoughts and actions.

In the light of this truth what,

then, is the meaning of "fighting against circumstances"? It means that a man is continually revolting against an *effect* without, while all the time he is nourishing and preserving its *cause* in his heart. That cause may take the form of a conscious vice or an unconscious weakness; but whatever it is, it stubbornly retards the efforts of its possessor, and thus calls aloud for remedy.

Men are anxious to improve their circumstances, but are unwilling to improve themselves; they therefore remain bound. The man who does not shrink from self-crucifixion can never fail to accomplish the object upon which his heart is set. This is as true of earthly as of heavenly things. Even the man whose sole object is to acquire wealth must be prepared to make great personal sacrifices before he can accomplish his object; and how much more so he who would realise a strong and well-poised life?

Here is a man who is wretchedly poor. He is extremely anxious that his surroundings and home comforts should be improved, yet all the time he shirks his work, and considers he is justified in trying to deceive his employer on the ground of the insufficiency of his wages. Such a man does not understand the simplest rudiments of those principles which are the basis of true prosperity, and is not only totally unfitted to rise out of his wretchedness, but is actually attracting to himself a still deeper wretchedness by dwelling in, and acting out, indolent, deceptive, and unmanly thoughts.

Here is a rich man who is the victim of a painful and persistent disease as the result of gluttony. He is willing to give large sums of money to get rid of it, but he will not sacrifice his gluttonous desires. He wants to gratify his taste for rich and unnatural viands and have his health as well. Such a man is totally unfit to have health, because he has not yet learned the first principles of a healthy life.

Here is an employer of labour who adopts crooked measures to avoid paying the regulation wage, and, in the hope of making larger profits, reduces the wages of his work-people. Such a man is altogether unfitted for prosperity, and when he finds himself bankrupt, both as regards reputation and riches, he blames circumstances, not knowing that he is the sole author of his condition.

I have introduced these three cases merely as illustrative of the truth that man is the causer (though nearly always unconsciously) of his circumstances, and that, whilst aiming at a good end, he is continually frustrating its accomplishment by encouraging thoughts and desires which cannot possibly harmonise with that end. Such cases could be multiplied and varied almost indefinitely, but this is not necessary, as the reader can, if he so resolves, trace the action of the laws of thought in his own mind and life, and until this is done, mere external facts cannot serve as a ground of reasoning.

Circumstances, however, are so complicated, thought is so deeply rooted, and the conditions of happiness vary so vastly with individuals, that a man's *entire* soul-condition (although it may be known to himself) cannot be judged by another from the external aspect of his life alone. A man may be honest in certain directions, yet suffer privations; a man may be dishonest in certain directions, yet acquire wealth; but the conclusion usually formed that the one man fails *because of his particular honesty,* and that the other prospers *because of his particular dishonesty,* is the result of a superficial judgment, which assumes that the dishonest man is almost totally corrupt, and the honest man almost entirely virtuous. In the light of a deeper knowledge and wider experience, such judgment is found to be erroneous. The dishonest man

may have some admirable virtues
which the other does not possess; and
the honest man obnoxious vices which
are absent in the other. The honest
man reaps the good results of his
honest thoughts and acts; he also
brings upon himself the sufferings
which his vices produce. The dishonest man likewise garners his own
suffering and happiness.

It is pleasing to human vanity to
believe that one suffers because of
one's virtue; but not until a man has
extirpated every sickly, bitter, and
impure thought from his mind, and
washed every sinful stain from his
soul, can he be in a position to know
and declare that his sufferings are
the result of his good, and not of his
bad qualities; and on the way to, yet
long before he has reached, that su-

preme perfection, he will have found, working in his mind and life, the Great Law which is absolutely just, and which cannot, therefore, give good for evil, evil for good. Possessed of such knowledge, he will then know, looking back upon his past ignorance and blindness, that his life is, and always was, justly ordered, and that all his past experiences, good and bad, were the equitable outworking of his evolving, yet unevolved self.

Good thoughts and actions can never produce bad results; bad thoughts and actions can never produce good results. This is but saying that nothing can come from corn but corn, nothing from nettles but nettles. Men understand this law in the natural world, and work with it; but few understand it in the mental and moral world (though its operation there is just as simple and undeviating), and they, therefore, do not co-operate with it.

Suffering is *always* the effect of wrong thought in some direction. It is an indication that the individual is out of harmony with himself, with the Law of his being. The sole and supreme use of suffering is to purify, to burn out all that is useless and impure. Suffering ceases for him who is pure. There could be no object in burning gold after the dross had been removed, and a perfectly pure and enlightened being could not suffer.

The circumstances which a man encounters with suffering are the result of his own mental inharmony. The circumstances which a man encounters with blessedness are the result of his own mental harmony. Blessedness, not material possessions, is the measure of right thought; wretchedness, not lack of material possessions, is the measure of wrong thought. A man may be cursed and rich; he may be blessed and poor. Blessedness and riches are only joined together when the riches are rightly and wisely used; and the poor man only descends into wretchedness when he regards his lot as a burden unjustly imposed.

Indigence and indulgence are the two extremes of wretchedness. They are both equally unnatural and the result of mental disorder. A man is not rightly conditioned until he is a happy, healthy, and prosperous being; and happiness, health, and prosperity are the result of a harmonious adjust-

ment of the inner with the outer, of
the man with his surroundings.

A man only begins to be a man
when he ceases to whine and revile,
and commences to search for the
hidden justice which regulates his life.
And as he adapts his mind to that
regulating factor, he ceases to accuse
others as the cause of his condition,
and builds himself up in strong and
noble thoughts; ceases to kick against
circumstances, but begins to *use* them
as aids to his more rapid progress,
and as a means of discovering the
hidden powers and possibilities within
himself.

Law, not confusion, is the dominat-
ing principle in the universe; justice,
not injustice, is the soul and sub-
stance of life; and righteousness, not
corruption, is the moulding and mov-

ing force in the spiritual government of the world. This being so, man has but to right himself to find that the universe is right; and during the process of putting himself right, he will find that as he alters his thoughts towards things and other people, things and other people will alter towards him.

The proof of this truth is in every person, and it therefore admits of easy investigation by systematic introspection and self-analysis. Let a man radically alter his thoughts, and he will be astonished at the rapid transformation it will effect in the material conditions of his life. Men imagine that thought can be kept secret, but it cannot; it rapidly crystallises into habit, and habit solidifies into circumstance. Bestial thoughts crystallise into

habits of drunkenness and sensuality,
which solidify into circumstances of
destitution and disease; impure
thoughts of every kind crystallise
into enervating and confusing habits,
which solidify into distracting and
adverse circumstances; thoughts of
fear, doubt, and indecision crystallise
into weak, unmanly, and irresolute
habits, which solidify into circumstances of failure, indigence, and
slavish dependence; lazy thoughts crystallise into habits of uncleanliness
and dishonesty, which solidify into
circumstances of foulness and beg-
gary; hateful and condemnatory
thoughts crystallise into habits of
accusation and violence, which solidify
into circumstances of injury and per
secution; selfish thoughts of all kinds
crystallise into habits of self-seeking,

which solidify into circumstances more
or less distressing. On the other
hand, beautiful thoughts of all kinds
crystallise into habits of grace and
kindliness, which solidify into genial
and sunny circumstances; pure
thoughts crystallise into habits of
temperance and self-control, which
solidify into circumstances of repose
and peace; thoughts of courage, self-
reliance, and decision crystallise into
manly habits, which solidify into circumstances of success, plenty, and
freedom; energetic thoughts crystallise
into habits of cleanliness and industry,
which solidify into circumstances of
pleasantness; gentle and forgiving
thoughts crystallise into habits of
gentleness, which solidify into protec-
tive and preservative circumstances;
loving and unselfish thoughts crystal-

lise into habits of self-forgetfulness for others, which solidify into circumstances of sure and abiding prosperity and true riches.

A particular train of thought persisted in, be it good or bad, cannot fail to produce its results on the character and circumstances. A man cannot *directly* choose his circumstances, but he can choose his thoughts, and so indirectly, yet surely, shape his circumstances.

Nature helps every man to the gratification of the thoughts which he most encourages, and opportunities are presented which will most speedily bring to the surface both the good and evil thoughts.

Let a man cease from his sinful thoughts, and all the world will soften towards him, and be ready to help

him; let him put away his weakly and
sickly thoughts, and lo! opportunities
will spring up on every hand to aid
his strong resolves; let him encourage
good thoughts, and no hard fate shall
bind him down to wretchedness and
shame. The world is your kaleido-
scope, and the varying combinations
of colours which at every succeeding
moment it presents to you are the
exquisitely adjusted pictures of your
ever-moving thoughts.

"You will be what you will to be;
    Let failure find its false content
    In that poor word 'environment,'
But spirit scorns it, and is free.

"It masters time, it conquers space;
    It cows that boastful trickster,
        Chance,
    And bids the tyrant Circumstance
Uncrown, and fill a servant's place.

" The human Will, that force unseen,
     The offspring of a deathless Soul,
     Can hew a way to any goal,
Though walls of granite intervene.

" Be not impatient in delay,
     But wait as one who understands;
     When spirit rises and commands,
The gods are ready to obey."

EFFECT OF THOUGHT ON
HEALTH AND THE BODY

THE body is the servant of the mind.
It obeys the operations of the
mind, whether they be deliberately
chosen or automatically expressed.
At the bidding of unlawful thoughts
the body sinks rapidly into disease
and decay; at the command of glad
and beautiful thoughts it becomes
clothed with youthfulness and beauty.
Disease and health, like circumstances, are rooted in thought. Sickly
thoughts will express themselves
through a sickly body. Thoughts of
fear have been known to kill a man

as speedily as a bullet, and they are
continually killing thousands of people just as surely though less rapidly.
The people who live in fear of disease are the people who get it. Anxiety quickly demoralises the whole
body, and lays it open to the entrance
of disease; while impure thoughts,
even if not physically indulged, will
soon shatter the nervous system.

Strong, pure, and happy thoughts
build up the body in vigour and grace.
The body is a delicate and plastic in-
strument, which responds readily to
the thoughts by which it is impressed,
and habits of thought will produce
their own effects, good or bad, upon it.

Men will continue to have impure
and poisoned blood, so long as they
propagate unclean thoughts. Out of
a clean heart comes a clean life and

a clean body. Out of a defiled mind
proceeds a defiled life and a corrupt
body. Thought is the fount of action,
life, and manifestation; make the fountain pure, and all will be pure.

Change of diet will not help a man
who will not change his thoughts.
When a man makes his thoughts pure,
he no longer desires impure food.

Clean thoughts make clean habits.
The so-called saint who does not
wash his body is not a saint. He
who has strengthened and purified his
thoughts does not need to consider
the malevolent microbe.

If you would perfect your body,
guard your mind. If you would re-
new your body, beautify your mind.
Thoughts of malice, envy, disappoint-
ment, despondency, rob the body of
its health and grace. A sour face

does not come by chance; it is made by sour thoughts. Wrinkles that mar are drawn by folly, passion, pride.

I know a woman of ninety-six who has the bright, innocent face of a girl. I know a man well under middle age whose face is drawn into inharmonious contours. The one is the result of a sweet and sunny disposition; the other is the outcome of passion and discontent.

As you cannot have a sweet and wholesome abode unless you admit the air and sunshine freely into your rooms, so a strong body and a bright, happy, or serene countenance can only result from the free admittance into the mind of thoughts of joy and goodwill and serenity.

On the faces of the aged there are wrinkles made by sympathy, others by strong and pure thought, and others are carved by passion: who cannot distinguish them? With those who have lived righteously, age is calm, peaceful, and softly mellowed, like the setting sun. I have recently seen a philosopher on his death-bed. He was not old except in years. He died as sweetly and peacefully as he had lived.

There is no physician like cheerful thought for dissipating the ills of the body; there is no comforter to compare with good-will for dispersing the shadows of grief and sorrow. To live continually in thoughts of ill-will, cynicism, suspicion, and envy, is to be confined in a self-made prison-hole. But to think well of all, to be cheerful with all, to patiently learn to find the good in all—such unselfish thoughts are the very portals of heaven; and to dwell day by day in thoughts of peace toward every creature will bring abounding peace to their possessor.

THOUGHT AND PURPOSE

UNTIL thought is linked with purpose there is no intelligent accomplishment. With the majority the bark of thought is allowed to "drift" upon the ocean of life. Aimlessness is a vice, and such drifting must not continue for him who would steer clear of catastrophe and destruction.

They who have no central purpose in their life fall an easy prey to petty worries, fears, troubles, and self-pityings, all of which are indications of weakness, which lead, just as surely as deliberately planned sins (though by a different route), to failure, unhappiness, and loss, for weakness cannot persist in a power-evolving universe.

A man should conceive of a legitimate purpose in his heart, and set out to accomplish it. He should make this purpose the centralising point of his thoughts. It may take the form of a spiritual ideal, or it may be a worldly object, according to his nature at the time being; but whichever it is, he should steadily focus his thought-forces upon the object which he has set before him. He should make this purpose his supreme duty, and should devote himself to its attainment, not allowing his thoughts to wander away into ephemeral fancies, longings, and imaginings. This is the royal road to self-control and true concentration of thought. Even if he

fails again and again to accomplish
his purpose (as he necessarily must
until weakness is overcome), the
strength of character gained will be
the measure of his *true* success, and
this will form a new starting-point for
future power and triumph.

Those who are not prepared for the
apprehension of a *great* purpose, should
fix the thoughts upon the faultless performance of their duty, no matter how
insignificant their task may appear.
Only in this way can the thoughts be
gathered and focussed, and resolution
and energy be developed, which being
done, there is nothing which may not
be accomplished.

The weakest soul, knowing its own
weakness, and believing this truth—
*that strength can only be developed
by effort and practice,* will, thus be-

lieving, at once begin to exert itself, and, adding effort to effort, patience to patience, and strength to strength, will never cease to develop, and will at last grow divinely strong.

As the physically weak man can make himself strong by careful and patient training, so the man of weak thoughts can make them strong by exercising himself in right thinking.

To put away aimlessness and weakness, and to begin to think with purpose, is to enter the ranks of those strong ones who only recognise failure as one of the pathways to attainment; who make all conditions serve them, and who think strongly, attempt fearlessly, and accomplish masterfully.

Having conceived of his purpose, a man should mentally mark out a *straight* pathway to its achievement, looking neither to the right nor to the left. Doubts and fears should be rigorously excluded; they are disintegrating elements which break up the straight line of effort, rendering it crooked, ineffectual, useless. Thoughts of doubt and fear never accomplish anything, and never can. They always lead to failure. Purpose, energy, power to do, and all strong thoughts cease when doubt and fear creep in.

The will to do springs from the knowledge that we *can* do. Doubt and fear are the great enemies of knowledge, and he who encourages them, who does not slay them, thwarts himself at every step.

He who has conquered doubt and fear has conquered failure. His every thought is allied with power, and all difficulties are bravely met and wisely overcome. His purposes are seasonably planted, and they bloom and bring forth fruit which does not fall prematurely to the ground.

Thought allied fearlessly to purpose becomes creative force; he who *knows* this is ready to become something higher and stronger than a mere bundle of wavering thoughts and fluctuating sensations; he who *does* this has become the conscious and intelligent wielder of his mental powers.

THE THOUGHT-FACTOR IN ACHIEVEMENT

ALL that a man achieves and all that he fails to achieve is the direct result of his own thoughts. In a justly ordered universe, where loss of equipoise would mean total destruction, individual responsibility must be absolute. A man's weakness and strength, purity and impurity, are his own, and not another man's; they are brought about by himself, and not by another; and they can only be altered by himself, never by another. His condition is also his own, and not another man's. His suffering and his happiness are evolved from within. As he thinks, so he is; as he continues to think, so he remains.

A strong man cannot help a weaker unless that weaker is *willing* to be helped, and even then the weak man must become strong of himself; he must, by his own efforts, develop the strength which he admires in another. None but himself can alter his condition.

It has been usual for men to think and to say, "Many men are slaves because one is an oppressor; let us hate the oppressor." Now, however, there is amongst an increasing few a tendency to reverse this judgment, and to say, "One man is an oppressor because many are slaves; let us despise the slaves." The truth is that oppressor and slave are co-operators in ignorance, and, while seeming to afflict each other, are in reality afflicting themselves. A perfect Knowledge perceives the action of law in the weakness of the oppressed and the misapplied power of the oppressor; a perfect Love, seeing the suffering which both states entail, condemns neither; a perfect Compassion embraces both oppressor and oppressed.

He who has conquered weakness, and has put away all selfish thoughts, belongs neither to oppressor nor oppressed. He is free.

A man can only rise, conquer, and achieve by lifting up his thoughts. He can only remain weak, and abject, and miserable by refusing to lift up his thoughts.

Before a man can achieve anything,

even in worldly things, he must lift
his thoughts above slavish animal indulgence. He may not, in order to
succeed, give up *all* animality and
selfishness, by any means; but a por-
tion of it must, at least, be sacrificed.
A man whose first thought is bestial
indulgence could neither think clearly
nor plan methodically; he could not
find and develop his latent resources,
and would fail in any undertaking.
Not having commenced to manfully
control his thoughts, he is not in a
position to control affairs and to
adopt serious responsibilities. He is
not fit to act independently and stand
alone. But he is limited only by the
thoughts which he chooses.

There can be no progress, no achievement without sacrifice, and a man's
worldly success will be in the measure

that he sacrifices his confused animal thoughts, and fixes his mind on the development of his plans, and the strengthening of his resolution and self-reliance. And the higher he lifts his thoughts, the more manly, upright, and righteous he becomes, the greater will be his success, the more blessed and enduring will be his achievements.

The universe does not favour the greedy, the dishonest, the vicious, although on the mere surface it may sometimes appear to do so; it helps the honest, the magnanimous, the virtuous. All the great Teachers of the ages have declared this in varying forms, and to prove and know it a man has but to persist in making himself more and more virtuous by lifting up his thoughts.

Intellectual achievements are the re-

sult of thought consecrated to the
search for knowledge, or for the
beautiful and true in life and nature.
Such achievements may be sometimes
connected with vanity and ambition,
but they are not the outcome of those
characteristics; they are the natural
outgrowth of long and arduous effort,
and of pure and unselfish thoughts.

Spiritual achievements are the con-
summation of holy aspirations. He
who lives constantly in the conception
of noble and lofty thoughts, who dwells
upon all that is pure and unselfish,
will, as surely as the sun reaches its
zenith and the moon its full, become
wise and noble in character, and rise
into a position of influence and
blessedness.

Achievement, of whatever kind, is
the crown of effort, the diadem of

thought. By the aid of self-control, resolution, purity, righteousness, and well-directed thought a man ascends; by the aid of animality, indolence, impurity, corruption, and confusion of thought a man descends.

A man may rise to high success in the world, and even to lofty altitudes in the spiritual realm, and again descend into weakness and wretchedness by allowing arrogant, selfish, and corrupt thoughts to take possession of him.

Victories attained by right thought can only be maintained by watchfulness. Many give way when success is assured, and rapidly fall back into failure.

All achievements, whether in the business, intellectual, or spiritual world, are the result of definitely directed thought, are governed by the same law, and are of the same method; the only difference lies in *the object of attainment.*

He who would accomplish little must sacrifice little; he who would achieve much must sacrifice much; he who would attain highly must sacrifice greatly.

VISIONS AND IDEALS

THE dreamers are the saviours of the world. As the visible world is sustained by the invisible, so men, through all their trials and sins and sordid vocations, are nourished by the beautiful visions of their solitary dreamers. Humanity cannot forget its dreamers; it cannot let their ideals fade and die; it lives in them; it knows them as the *realities* which it shall one day see and know.

Composer, sculptor, painter, poet, prophet, sage, these are the makers of the after-world, the architects of heaven. The world is beautiful because they have lived; without them, labouring humanity would perish.

He who cherishes a beautiful vision, a lofty ideal in his heart, will one day realise it. Columbus cherished a vision of another world, and he discovered it; Copernicus fostered the vision of a multiplicity of worlds and a wider universe, and he revealed it; Buddha beheld the vision of a spiritual world of stainless beauty and perfect peace, and he entered into it.

Cherish your visions; cherish your ideals; cherish the music that stirs in your heart, the beauty that forms in your mind, the loveliness that drapes your purest thoughts, for out of them will grow all delightful conditions, all heavenly environment; of these, if you but remain true to them, your world will at last be built.

To desire is to obtain; to aspire is to achieve. Shall man's basest desires receive the fullest measure of gratification, and his purest aspirations starve for lack of sustenance? Such is not the Law: such a condition of things can never obtain: "Ask and receive."

Dream lofty dreams, and as you dream, so shall you become. Your Vision is the promise of what you shall one day be; your Ideal is the prophecy of what you shall at last unveil.

The greatest achievement was at first and for a time a dream. The oak sleeps in the acorn; the bird waits in the egg; and in the highest vision of the soul a waking angel stirs. Dreams are the seedlings of realities.

Your circumstances may be uncon-

genial, but they shall not long remain so if you but perceive an Ideal
and strive to reach it. You cannot
travel *within* and stand still *without*.
Here is a youth hard pressed by
poverty and labour; confined long
hours in an unhealthy workshop; un-
schooled, and lacking all the arts of
refinement. But he dreams of better
things; he thinks of intelligence, of
refinement, of grace and beauty. He
conceives of, mentally builds up, an
ideal condition of life; the vision of
a wider liberty and a larger scope
takes possession of him; unrest urges
him to action, and he utilises all his
spare time and means, small though
they are, to the development of his
latent powers and resources. Very
soon so altered has his mind become
that the workshop can no longer hold

him. It has become so out of harmony with his mentality that it falls
out of his life as a garment is cast
aside, and, with the growth of opportunities which fit the scope of his
expanding powers, he passes out of it
forever. Years later we see this
youth as a full-grown man. We find
him a master of certain forces of the
mind which he wields with world-wide
influence and almost unequalled power.
In his hands he holds the cords of
gigantic responsibilities; he speaks,
and lo! lives are changed; men and
women hang upon his words and re-
mould their characters, and, sunlike,
he becomes the fixed and luminous
centre round which innumerable de-
stinies revolve. He has realised the
Vision of his youth. He has become
one with his Ideal.

And you, too, youthful reader, will realise the Vision (not the idle wish) of your heart, be it base or beautiful, or a mixture of both, for you will always gravitate toward that which you, secretly, most love. Into your hands will be placed the exact results of your own thoughts; you will receive that which you earn; no more, no less. Whatever your present environment may be, you will fall, remain, or rise with your thoughts, your Vision, your Ideal. You will become as small as your controlling desire; as great as your dominant aspiration: in the beautiful words of Stanton Davis Kirkham, " You may be keeping accounts, and presently you shall walk out of the door that for so long has seemed to you the barrier of your ideals, and shall find yourself

before an audience—the pen still behind your ear, the inkstains on your
fingers—and then and there shall pour
out the torrent of your inspiration.
You may be driving sheep, and you
shall wander to the city—bucolic and
open-mouthed; shall wander under the
intrepid guidance of the spirit into
the studio of the master, and after a
time he shall say, 'I have nothing
more to teach you.' And now you
have become the master, who did so
recently dream of great things while
driving sheep. You shall lay down
the saw and the plane to take upon
yourself the regeneration of the world."

The thoughtless, the ignorant, and
the indolent, seeing only the apparent
effects of things and not the things
themselves, talk of luck, of fortune,
and chance. Seeing a man grow rich,

they say, "How lucky he is!" Observing another become intellectual, they exclaim, "How highly favoured he is!" And noting the saintly character and wide influence of another, they remark, "How chance aids him at every turn!" They do not see the trials and failures and struggles which these men have voluntarily encountered in order to gain their experience; have no knowledge of the sacrifices they have made, of the undaunted efforts they have put forth, of the faith they have exercised, that they might overcome the apparently insurmountable, and realise the Vision of their heart. They do not know the darkness and the heartaches; they only see the light and joy, and call it "luck"; do not see the long and arduous journey, but only behold the pleasant goal, and call it "good fortune"; do not understand the process, but only perceive the result, and call it "chance."

In all human affairs there are *efforts,* and there are *results,* and the strength of the effort is the measure of the result. Chance is not. "Gifts," powers, material, intellectual, and spiritual possessions are the fruits of effort; they are thoughts completed, objects accomplished, visions realised.

The Vision that you glorify in your mind, the Ideal that you enthrone in your heart—this you will build your life by, this you will become.

SERENITY

CALMNESS of mind is one of the beautiful jewels of wisdom. It is the result of long and patient effort in self-control. Its presence is an indication of ripened experience, and of a more than ordinary knowledge of the laws and operations of thought.

A man becomes calm in the measure that he understands himself as a thought-evolved being, for such knowledge necessitates the understanding of others as the result of thought, and as he develops a right understanding, and sees more and more clearly the internal relations of things by the action of cause and effect, he ceases to fuss and fume and worry and grieve, and remains poised, steadfast, serene.

The calm man, having learned how to govern himself, knows how to adapt himself to others; and they, in turn, reverence his spiritual strength, and feel that they can learn of him and rely upon him. The more tranquil a man becomes, the greater is his success, his influence, his power for good. Even the ordinary trader will find his business prosperity increase as he develops a greater self-control and equanimity, for people will always prefer to deal with a man whose demeanour is strongly equable.

The strong, calm man is always loved and revered. He is like a shade-giving tree in a thirsty land, or a sheltering rock in a storm. "Who does not love a tranquil heart, a sweet-tempered, balanced life? It does not matter whether it rains or shines, or what changes come to those possessing these blessings, for they are always sweet, serene, and calm. That exquisite poise of character which we call serenity is the last lesson of culture; it is the flowering of life, the fruitage of the soul. It is precious as wisdom, more to be desired than gold—yea, than even fine gold. How insignificant mere money-seeking looks in comparison with a serene life—a life that dwells in the ocean of Truth, beneath the waves, beyond the reach of tempests, in the Eternal Calm!

"How many people we know who sour their lives, who ruin all that is sweet and beautiful by explosive tem-

pers, who destroy their poise of character, and make bad blood! It is a
question whether the great majority
of people do not ruin their lives and
mar their happiness by lack of self-
control. How few people we meet in
life who are well balanced, who have
that exquisite poise which is charac-
teristic of the finished character!"

Yes, humanity surges with uncon-
trolled passion, is tumultuous with
ungoverned grief, is blown about by
anxiety and doubt. Only the wise
man, only he whose thoughts are controlled and purified, makes the winds
and the storms of the soul obey him.

Tempest-tossed souls, wherever ye
may be, under whatsoever conditions
ye may live, know this—in the ocean
of life the isles of Blessedness are
smiling, and the sunny shore of your

ideal awaits your coming. Keep your hand firmly upon the helm of thought. In the bark of your soul reclines the commanding Master; He does but sleep: wake Him.   Self-control is strength; Right Thought is mastery; Calmness is power. Say unto your heart, " Peace, be still!"

Out from the Heart

FOREWORD

CONFUCIUS said, " The perfecting of one's self is the fundamental base of all progress and all moral development"; a maxim as profound and comprehensive as it is simple, practical, and uninvolved, for there is no surer way to knowledge, nor no better way to help the world than by perfecting one's self. Nor is there any nobler work or higher science than that of self-perfection. He who studies how to become faultless, who strives to be pure-hearted, who aims at the possession of a calm, wise, and seeing mind, engages in the most sublime task that man can undertake, and the results of which are perceptible in a well-ordered, blessed, and beautiful life.

JAMES ALLEN

THE HEART AND THE LIFE

AS the heart, so is the life. The within is ceaselessly becoming the without. Nothing remains un-revealed. That which is hidden is but for a time; it ripens and comes forth at last. Seed, tree, blossom, and fruit is the fourfold order of the universe. From the state of a man's heart pro-ceed the conditions of his life; his thoughts blossom into deeds, and his deeds bear the fruitage of character and destiny.

Life is ever unfolding from within,

and revealing itself to the light, and
thoughts engendered in the heart at
last reveal themselves in words, actions, and things accomplished.

As the fountain from the hidden
spring, so issues man's life from the
secret recesses of his heart. All that
he is and does is generated there. All
that he will be and do will take its
rise there.

Sorrow and gladness, suffering and
enjoyment, hope and fear, hatred and
love, ignorance and enlightenment, are
nowhere but in the heart; they are
solely mental conditions.

Man is the keeper of his heart; the
watcher of his mind; the solitary sen-
tinel of his citadel of life. As such,
he can be diligent or negligent. He
can keep his heart more and more
carefully; he can more strenuously

watch and purify his mind; and he
can guard himself against the thinking of unrighteous thoughts; this is the
way of enlightenment and bliss. On
the other hand, he can live loosely and
carelessly, neglecting the supreme task
of rightly ordering his life: this is
the way of self-delusion and suffering.

Let a man realise that life in its
totality proceeds from the mind, and
lo, the way of blessedness is opened
up to him! For he will then discover
that he possesses the power to rule his
mind, and to fashion it in accordance
with his ideal. So will he elect to
strongly and steadfastly walk those
pathways of thought and action which
are altogether excellent; to him life
will become beautiful and sacred; and,
sooner or later, he will put to flight
all evil, confusion, and suffering; for,

it is impossible for a man to fall
short of liberation, enlightenment, and
peace, who guards with unwearying
diligence the gateway of his heart.

THE NATURE AND POWER
OF MIND

MIND is the arbiter of life; it is the creator and shaper of conditions, and the recipient of its own results. It contains within itself both the power to create illusion and to perceive reality.

Mind is the infallible weaver of destiny; thought is the thread, good and evil deeds are the warp and woof, and the web, woven upon the loom of life, is character. Mind clothes itself in garments of its own making.

Man, as a mental being, possesses all

the powers of mind, and is furnished with illimitable choice. He learns by experience, and he can accelerate or retard his experience. He is not arbitrarily bound at any point, but he has bound himself at many points, and having bound himself he can, when he chooses, liberate himself. He can become bestial or pure, ignoble or noble, foolish or wise, just as he chooses. He can, by recurring practice, form habits, and he can, by renewed effort, break them off. He can surround himself with illusions until Truth is completely lost, and he can destroy one and another of those illusions until Truth is entirely recovered. His possibilities are limitless; his freedom is complete.

It is in the nature of mind to create its own conditions, and to choose the states in which it shall dwell. It also has the power to alter any condition and to abandon any state, and this it is continually doing as it gathers knowledge of state after state by repeated choice and exhaustive experience.

Inward processes of thought make up the sum of character and life, and man can modify and alter these processes by bringing will and effort to bear upon them. The bonds of habit, impotence, and sin are self-made, and can only be destroyed by one's self; they exist nowhere but in one's mind, and although they are directly related to outward things, they have no real existence in those things. The outer is moulded and vivified by the inner, and never the inner by the outer. Temptation does not arise in the outer object, but *in the lust of the mind for that object;* nor do suffering and sorrow inhere in the external things and happenings of life, but in an undisciplined attitude of mind toward those things and happenings. The mind that is disciplined by Purity and fortified by Wisdom, avoids all those lusts and desires which are inseparably bound up with affliction, and so arrives at enlightenment and peace.

To condemn others as evil, and to rail against outside conditions as the source of evil, increases, and does not lessen, the world's suffering and unrest. The outer is but the shadow and effect of the inner, and when the heart is pure all outward things are pure.

All growth and life is from within outward; all decay and death is from

without inward; this is a universal
law. All evolution proceeds from
within. All adjustment must take
place within. He who ceases to strive
against others, and employs his powers in the transformation, regeneration, and development of his own
mind, conserves his energies and pre-
serves himself; and as he succeeds in
harmonising his own mind, he leads
others by consideration and charity
into a like blessed state, for not by
assuming authority and guidance over
other minds is the way of enlightenment and peace discovered, but by exercising a lawful authority over one's
own, and by guiding one's self in pathways of steadfast and lofty virtue.

A man's life proceeds from his heart,
his mind: he has compounded that
mind by his own thoughts and deeds;

it is in his power to refashion that
mind by his choice of thought; he can
therefore transform his life. Let us
see how this is to be done.

FORMATION OF HABIT

EVERY established mental condition is an *acquired habit,* and it has become such by continuous repetition of thought. Despondency and cheerfulness, anger and calmness, covetousness and generosity—indeed, all states of mind—are habits built up by choice, until they have become automatic. A thought constantly repeated at last becomes a fixed habit of the mind, and from such habits proceeds the life.

It is in the nature of the mind to acquire knowledge by the repetition of its experiences. A thought which it is very difficult, at first, to hold and to dwell upon, at last becomes, by constantly being held in the mind, a natural and habitual condition. Just as a boy, when commencing to learn a trade, cannot even handle his tools aright, much less use them correctly, but after long repetition and practice plies them with perfect ease and consummate skill, so a state of mind, at first apparently impossible of realisation, is, by perseverance and practice, at last acquired and built into the character as a natural and spontaneous condition.

In this power of the mind to form and re-form its habits, its conditions, is contained the basis of man's salvation, and the open door to perfect liberty by the mastery of self, for as a man has the power to form harmful habits, so he has the same power to create habits that are essentially good. And here we come to a point which needs some elucidating, and which calls for deep and earnest thought on the part of my reader.

It is commonly said to be easier to do wrong than right, to sin than to be holy; such condition has come to be regarded, almost universally, as axiomatic, and no less a teacher than the Buddha has said:—" Bad deeds, and deeds hurtful to ourselves, are easy to do; what is beneficial and good, that is very difficult to do,"—and as regards humanity generally, this is true, but it is only true as a passing experience, a fleeting factor in human evolution; it is not a fixed condition of things, is not of the nature of an eternal truth. It is easier for men to do wrong than right, because of the prevalence of *ignorance,* because the true nature of things, and the essence and meaning of life, are not apprehended. When a child is learning to write, it is extremely easy for it to hold the pen wrongly, and to form its letters incorrectly, but it is painfully difficult to hold the pen and to write properly; and this because of the child's ignorance of the art of writing, which can only be dispelled by persistent effort and practice, until, at last, it becomes natural and easy to hold the pen properly, and to write correctly, and difficult, as well as altogether unnecessary, to do the wrong thing. It is the same in the vital things of mind and life. To think and do rightly requires much practice and renewed effort, but the time at last

comes when it becomes habitual and
easy to think and do rightly, and difficult, as it is then seen to be altogether unnecessary, to do that which
is wrong.

Just as an artisan becomes, by practice, accomplished in his craft, so a
man can become, by practice, accomplished in goodness; it is entirely a
matter of forming new habits of
thought, and he to whom right
thoughts have become easy and natural, and wrong thoughts and acts
difficult to do, has attained to the
highest virtue, to pure, spiritual
knowledge.

It is easy and natural for men to
sin, because they have formed, by incessant repetition, harmful and unenlightened habits of thought. It is very
difficult for the thief to refrain from

stealing when opportunity occurs, because he has lived so long in covetous
and avaricious thoughts; but such dif-
ficulty does not exist for the honest
man who has lived so long in upright
and honest thoughts, and has thereby
become enlightened as to the wrong,
folly, and fruitlessness of theft, that
even the remotest idea of stealing does
not enter his mind. The sin of theft
is a very extreme one, and I have introduced it in order to the more
clearly illustrate the force and for-
mation of habit; but all sins and
virtues are formed in the same way.
Anger and impatience are natural and
easy to thousands of people, because
they are constantly repeating the angry
and impatient thought and act, and
with each repetition the habit is more
firmly established and more deeply

rooted. Calmness and patience can
become habitual in the same way—by
first grasping, through effort, a calm
and patient thought, and then con-
tinuously thinking it, and living in it,
until " use becomes second nature," and
anger and impatience pass away forever. It is thus that every wrong
thought may be expelled from the
mind; thus that every untrue act may
be destroyed; thus that every sin may
be overcome.

DOING AND KNOWING

LET a man realise that his life, in its totality, proceeds from his mind, and that that mind is a combination of habits which he can, by patient effort, modify to any extent, and over which he can thus gain complete ascendency and control, and he has at once obtained possession of the key which shall open the door to his complete emancipation.

But emancipation from the ills of life (which are the ills of one's mind) is a matter of steady growth from within, and not a sudden acquisition from without. Hourly and daily must the mind be trained to think stainless thoughts, and to adopt right and dispassionate attitudes under those circumstances in which it is prone to fall into wrong and passion. Like the patient sculptor upon his marble, the aspirant to the Right Life must gradually work upon the crude material of his mind until he has wrought out of it the Ideal of his holiest dreams.

In working toward such supreme accomplishment, it is necessary to commence at the lowest and easiest steps, and proceed by natural and progressive stages to the higher and more difficult. This law of growth, progress, evolution, unfoldment, by gradual and ever ascending stages, is absolute in every department of life, and in every human accomplishment, and where it is ignored, total failure will result. In acquiring learning, in learning a trade, or in pursuing a business, this law is fully recognised and minutely obeyed by all; but in acquiring Virtue, in learning Truth, and in pursuing the right conduct and knowledge of life, it is unrecognised and disobeyed by nearly all; hence Virtue, Truth, and the Perfect Life remain unpractised, unacquired, and unknown.

It is a common error to suppose that the Higher Life is a matter of reading, and the adoption of theological or metaphysical hypotheses, and that Spiritual Principles can be apprehended by this method. The Higher Life is a *higher living* in thought, word, and deed, and the knowledge of those Spiritual Principles, which

are imminent in man and in the universe can only be acquired after long
discipline in the pursuit and practice
of Virtue.

The lesser must be thoroughly
grasped and understood before the
greater can be known, and practice
always precedes *real* knowledge. The
schoolmaster never attempts to teach
his pupils the abstract principles of
mathematics at the commencement; he
knows that by such a method teach-
ing would be vain, and learning impossible. He first places before them
a simple sum, and, having explained
it, leaves them to *do it*. When, after
repeated failures and ever-renewed
effort, they have succeeded in doing
it correctly, a more difficult task is
set them, and then another and another; and not until the pupils have,

through many years of diligent application, mastered all the lessons in arithmetic, does he attempt to unfold to them the underlying mathematical principles.

In learning a trade, say that of a mechanic, the boy is not at first taught the principles of mechanics, but a simple tool is put into his hand and he is told how rightly to use it, and is then left to do it by effort and practice. As he succeeds in plying his tools correctly, more and more difficult tasks are set him, until, after several years of successful practice, he is prepared to study and grasp the principles of mechanics.

In a properly governed household, the child is first taught to be obedient, and to conduct himself properly under all circumstances. The child is not even told why he must do this, but is commanded to do it, and only after he has so far succeeded in doing what is right and proper, is he told *why* he should do it. No father would attempt to teach his child the principles of ethics before exacting from him the practice of filial duty and social virtue.

Thus practice ever precedes knowledge even in the ordinary things of the world, and in spiritual things, in the living of the Higher Life, this law is rigid in its exactions. Virtue can only be known by *doing*, and the knowledge of Truth can only be arrived at by perfecting one's self in the practice of Virtue and to be complete in the practice and acquisition of Virtue is to be complete in the knowledge of Truth.

Truth can only be arrived at by daily and hourly doing the lessons of Virtue, beginning at the simplest, and passing on to the more difficult; and as a child patiently and obediently learns its lessons at school, constantly practising, ever exerting himself until all failures and difficulties are surmounted, even so does the child of Truth apply himself to right-doing in thought and action, undaunted by failure, and made stronger by difficulties; and as he succeeds in acquiring Virtue, his mind unfolds itself in the knowledge of Truth, and it is a knowledge in which he can securely rest.

FIRST STEPS IN THE HIGHER LIFE

SEEING that the Path of Virtue is the Path of Knowledge, and that before the all-embracing Principles of Truth can be comprehended, perfection in the more lowly steps must be acquired, how, then, shall a disciple of Truth commence? How shall one who aspires to the righting of his mind and the purification of his heart —that heart which is the fountain and repository of all the issues of life—learn the lessons of Virtue, and thus build himself up in the strength of knowledge, destroying ignorance

and the ills of life? What are the
first lessons, the first steps? How are
they learned? How are they practised? How are they mastered and
understood?

The first lessons consist in overcoming those wrong mental conditions
which are most easily eradicated,
and which are the common barriers
to spiritual progress, as well as in
practising the simple domestic and
social virtues; and the reader will be
the better aided if I group and classify
the first ten steps in three lessons as
follows:

VICES TO BE OVERCOME AND ERADICATED

Vices of the Body

1. Indolence.   } *First Lesson.*
2. Self-Indulgence. { Discipline of the Body.

Vices of the Tongue

1. Slander.
2. Gossip and idle con-
   versation.
3. Abusive and unkind
   speech.
4. Levity, or irreverent
   speech.
5. Captiousness, or fault-
   finding speech.

Second Lesson.
Discipline of
Speech.

Virtues to be Practised and Acquired

1. Unselfish performance
   of duty.
2. Unswerving rectitude.
3. Unlimited forgiveness.

Third Lesson.
Discipline of
Inclination.

The two vices of the body, and five
of the tongue, are so called because
they are manifested in the body and
tongue, and also because, by so definitely classifying them, the mind of
the reader will be the better helped;
but it must be clearly understood
that these vices arise primarily in the

mind, and are wrong conditions of
heart worked out in the body and the
tongue.

The existence of such chaotic conditions is an indication that the mind is
altogether unenlightened as to the real
meaning and purpose of life, and their
eradication is the beginning of a virtuous, steadfast, and enlightened life.

But how shall they be overcome and
eradicated? By first, and at once,
checking and controlling their outward manifestations, by suppressing
the wrong act; this will stimulate the
mind to watchfulness and reflection
until, by repeated practice, it will at
last come to perceive and understand
the dark and wrong conditions of
mind, out of which such acts spring,
and will abandon them entirely.

It will be seen that the first step

in the discipline of the mind is the
overcoming of indolence. This is the
easiest step, and until it is perfectly
accomplished, the other steps cannot
be taken. The clinging to indolence
constitutes a complete barrier to the
Path of Truth. Indolence consists in
giving the body more ease and sleep
than it requires, in procrastinating,
and in shirking and neglecting those
things which should receive immediate
attention. This condition of laziness
must be overcome by rousing up the
body at an early hour, giving it just
the amount of sleep it requires for
complete recuperation, and by doing
promptly and vigorously, every task
and duty, no matter how small, as it
comes along. On no account should
food or drink be taken in bed, and to
lie in bed after one has wakened, in-

dulging in ease and reverie, is a habit fatal to promptness and resolution of character, and purity of mind. Nor should one attempt to do his thinking at such a time. Strong, pure, and true thinking is impossible under such circumstances. A man should go to bed to sleep, not to think. He should get up to think and work, not to sleep.

The next step is the overcoming of self-indulgence, or gluttony. The glutton is he who eats for animal gratification only, without considering the true end and object in eating, who eats more than his body requires, and is greedy after sweet things and rich dishes. Such undisciplined desire can only be overcome by reducing the quantity of food eaten, and the number of meals per day, and by resorting to a simple and uninvolved dietary. Regular hours should be set apart for meals, and eating at other times should be rigidly avoided. Suppers should be abolished, as they are altogether unnecessary, and conduce to heavy sleep and cloudiness of mind. The pursuit of such a method of discipline will rapidly bring the hitherto ungoverned appetite under control, and as the sensual sin of self-indulgence is taken out of the mind, the right selection of food will be instinctively and infallibly adapted to the purified mental condition.

It should be well borne in mind that *change of heart* is the needful thing, and that any change of diet, which does not subserve this end is futile. Whilst one eats for enjoyment he is gluttonous. The heart must be purified of sensual craving and gustatory lust.

When the body is well controlled and firmly guided; when that which is to be done is done vigorously; when no task or duty is delayed; when early rising has become a delight; when frugality, temperance, and abstinence are firmly established; when one is contented with the food which is put before him, no matter how scanty and plain, and the craving for gustatory pleasure is at an end,—then are the first two steps in the Higher Life accomplished; then is the first great lesson in Truth learned. Thus is established in the heart the foundation of a poised, self-governed, virtuous life.

The next lesson is the lesson of Virtuous Speech, in which are five orderly steps. The first step is the overcoming of slander. Slander consists in inventing or repeating evil reports about others, in exposing and magnifying the faults of others, or of absent friends, and in introducing unworthy insinuations. The elements of thoughtlessness, cruelty, insincerity, and untruthfulness enter into every slanderous act. He who aims at the living of the right life will commence to check the cruel word of slander before it has gone forth from his lips and will then check and eliminate the insincere thought which gave rise to it. He will watch himself that he does not vilify any, and will refrain from disparaging and condemning the absent friend, whose face he has so recently kissed, whose hand he has shaken, or into whose face he has

smiled. He will not say of another
that which he dare not say to him.
Thus, coming at last to think sacredly
of the character and reputation of
others, he will destroy those wrong
conditions of mind which give rise to
slander.

The next step is the overcoming of
gossip and idle conversation. Idle
speech consists in talking about the
private affairs of others, in talking
merely to pass away the time, and in
engaging in aimless and irrelevant
conversation. Such an ungoverned
condition of speech is the outcome of
an ill-regulated mind. The man of
virtue will bridle his tongue, and thus
learn how rightly to govern the mind.
He will not let his tongue run idly
and foolishly, but will make his
speech strong and pure and will

either talk with a purpose or remain silent.

Abusive and unkind speech is the next vice to be overcome. The man who abuses and accuses others has himself wandered far from the Right Way. To hurl hard words and names at others is to sink deeply into folly. When a man is inclined to abuse and condemn others, let him restrain his tongue and look in upon himself. The virtuous man refrains from abuse and quarrelling, and employs only words that are useful, necessary, pure, and true.

The next step is the overcoming of levity, or irreverent speech. Light and frivolous talking; the repeating of coarse jokes; the telling of vulgar stories, having no other purpose than to raise an empty laugh; offensive familiarity, and the employment of

contemptuous and irreverent terms
when speaking to or of others, and
particularly of one's elders and those
who rank as one's teachers, guardians,
or superiors,—all this will be put away
by the love of Virtue and Truth.

Upon the altar of irreverence absent friends and companions are im-
molated for the passing excitement of
a momentary laugh, and all the sanc-
tity of life is sacrificed to the zest
for ridicule. When respect towards
others and the giving of reverence
where reverence is due are abandoned,
Virtue is abandoned. When modesty,
gravity, and dignity are eliminated
from speech and behaviour, Truth is
lost, yea, even its entrance gate is
hidden away and forgotten. Irreverence is degrading even in the young,
but when it accompanies grey hairs,

and appears in the demeanour of the preacher,—this is indeed a piteous spectacle; and when this can be imitated and followed after, then are the blind leading the blind, then have elders and preacher and people lost their way.

The virtuous man will be of grave and reverent speech; he will think and speak of the absent as he thinks and speaks of the dead—tenderly and sacredly; he will put away thoughtlessness, and watch that he does not sacrifice his dignity to gratify a passing impulse to lightness and frivolity. His mirth will be pure and innocent, and his voice will become subdued and musical, and his soul be filled with grace and sweetness as he succeeds in conducting himself as becomes a man of Truth.

The last step in the second lesson is the overcoming of captiousness, or fault-finding speech. This vice of the tongue consists in magnifying and harping on small or apparent faults, in foolish quibbling and hair-splitting, and in pursuing vain arguments based upon groundless suppositions, beliefs, and opinions. Life is short and real, and sin and sorrow and pain are not remedied by carping and contention. The man who is ever on the watch to catch at the words of others in order to contradict and controvert them, has yet to reach the higher way of holiness, the truer life of self-surrender. The man who is ever on the watch to check his own words in order to soften and purify them will find the higher way and the truer life; he will conserve his energies, main-

tain his composure of mind, and
preserve within himself the spirit of
Truth.

When the tongue is well controlled
and wisely subdued; when selfish im-
pulses and unworthy thoughts no
longer rush to the tongue demanding
utterance; when the speech has become harmless, pure, gentle, gracious,
and purposeful, and no word is uttered
but in sincerity and truth,—then are
the five steps in virtuous speech accomplished, then is the second great
lesson in Truth learned and mastered.

And now some will ask, " But why
all this discipline of the body and
restraint of the tongue? Surely the
Higher Life can be realised and known
without such strenuous labour, such
incessant effort and watchfulness?"
No, it cannot. In the spiritual as the

material, nothing is done without labour, and the higher cannot be known until the lower is fulfilled. Can a man make a table before he has learned how to handle a tool and drive a nail? And can a man fashion his mind in accordance with Truth before he has overcome the slavery of his body? As the intricate subtleties of language cannot be apprehended and wielded before the alphabet and the simplest words are mastered, neither can the deep subtleties of the mind be understood and purified before the A B C of right conduct is perfectly acquired. As for the labour involved —does not the youth joyfully and patiently submit himself to a seven-years' apprenticeship in order to master a craft? And does he not day by day carefully and faithfully carry

out every detail of his master's in-
structions, looking forward to the
time when, perfected through obedi-
ence and practice, he shall be himself
a master? Where is the man who
sincerely aims at excellence in music,
painting, literature, in any trade,
business, or profession who is not
willing to give his whole life to
the acquirement of his particular
perfection? Shall labour, then, be
considered where the very highest excellence is concerned—the excellence
of Truth? He who says, "The Path
which you point out is too difficult;
I must have Truth without labour,
salvation without effort," that man
will not find his way out of the con-
fusions and sufferings of self-hood; he
will not find the calm and well-forti-
fied mind and the wisely-ordered life.

His love is for ease and enjoyment, and not for Truth. He who, deep in his heart, adores Truth, and aspires to know it, will consider no labour too great to be undertaken, but will adopt it joyfully and pursue it patiently, and by perseverance in practice he will come to the knowledge of Truth.

The necessity for this preliminary discipline of the body and tongue will be the more clearly perceived when it is fully understood that all these wrong outward conditions are merely the expressions of wrong conditions of heart. An indolent body means an indolent mind; an ill-regulated tongue reveals an ill-regulated mind, and the process of remedying the manifested condition is really a method of rectifying the inward state. Moreover, the overcoming of these conditions is only a small part of what is really involved in the process. The ceasing from evil leads to, and is inseparably connected with, the practice of good. While a man is overcoming indolence and self-indulgence, he is really cultivating and developing the virtues of abstinence, temperance, punctuality, and self-denial, and is acquiring that strength, energy, and resolution which are indispensable to the successful accomplishment of the higher tasks. While he is overcoming the vices of speech, he is developing the virtues of truthfulness, sincerity, reverence, kindliness, and self-control, and is gaining that mental steadiness and fixedness of purpose, without which the remoter subtleties of the mind cannot be regulated, and the higher stages of conduct and enlightenment cannot be reached. Also, as he has to *do* right, his knowledge deepens, and his insight is intensified, and as the child's heart is glad when his school task is mastered, so with each victory achieved, the man of virtue experiences a bliss which the seeker after pleasure and excitement can never know.

And now we come to the third lesson in the Higher Life, which consists in practising and mastering in one's daily life, three great fundamental Virtues—(1) Unselfish Performance of Duty; (2) Unswerving Rectitude; and (3) Unlimited Forgiveness. Having prepared the mind by overcoming the more surface and chaotic conditions mentioned in the first two lessons, the striver after Virtue and Truth is now ready to enter upon

greater and more difficult tasks, and
to control and purify the deeper mo-
tives of the heart. Without the right
performance of duty, the higher virtues
cannot be known, and Truth cannot
be apprehended. Duty is generally
regarded as an irksome labour, a
compulsory something which must be
toiled through, or be in some way
circumvented. This way of regarding
Duty proceeds from a selfish condition
of mind, and a wrong understanding
of life. All duty should be regarded
as sacred, and its faithful and unselfish performance one of the leading
rules of conduct. All personal and
selfish considerations should be ex-
tracted and cast away from the doing
of one's duty, and when this is done,
Duty ceases to be irksome, and becomes joyful. Duty is only irksome

to him who craves some selfish enjoyment or benefit for himself. Let the man who is chafing under the irksomeness of his duty look to himself, and he will find that his wearisomeness proceeds, not from the duty itself, but from his selfish desire to escape it. He who neglects duty, be it great or small, or of a public or private nature, neglects Virtue; he who in his heart rebels against Duty, rebels against Virtue. When Duty has become a thing of love, and when every particular duty is done accurately, faithfully, and dispassionately, there is much subtle selfishness removed from the heart, and a great step is taken towards the heights of Truth. The virtuous man concentrates his mind on the perfect doing of his own duty, and does not interfere with the duty of an other.

The second step in the third lesson is the practice of Unswerving Rectitude. This Virtue must be firmly established in the mind, and so enter into every detail of man's life. All dishonesty, deception, trickery, and misrepresentation must be forever put away, and the heart be purged of every vestige of insincerity and subterfuge. The least swerving from the path of rectitude is a deviation from Virtue. There must be no extravagance and exaggeration of speech, but the simple truth should be stated. Engaging in deception, no matter how apparently insignificant, for vain-glory, or with the hope of personal advantage, is a state of delusion which one should make efforts to dispel. It

is demanded of the man of Virtue
that he shall not only practice the
most rigid honesty in thought, word,
and deed, but that he shall be exact
in his statements, omitting and adding nothing to the actual truth. In
thus shaping his mind to the principle
of Rectitude, he will gradually come
to deal with people and things in a
just and impartial spirit, considering
equity before himself, and viewing all
things with freedom from personal
bias, passion, and prejudice. When
the Virtue of Rectitude is fully practised, acquired, and comprehended, so
that all temptation to untruthfulness and insincerity has ceased, then
is the heart made purer and nobler,
then is character strengthened, and
knowledge enlarged, and life takes
on a new meaning and a new

power. Thus is the second step accomplished.

The third step is the practice of Unlimited Forgiveness. This consists in overcoming the sense of injury which springs from vanity, selfishness, and pride; and in exercising disinterested charity and large-heartedness towards all. Spite, retaliation, and revenge are so utterly ignoble, and so small and foolish, as to be altogether unworthy of being noticed or harboured. No one who fosters such conditions in his heart can lift himself above folly and suffering, and guide his life aright. Only by casting them away, and ceasing to be moved by them, can a man's eyes be opened to the true way in life; only by developing a forgiving and charitable spirit can he hope to approach and perceive the strength and beauty of a well-ordered life. In the heart of the strongly virtuous man no feeling of personal injury can arise; he has put away all retaliation, and has no enemies; and if men should constitute themselves his enemies, he will regard them kindly, understanding their ignorance, and making full allowance for it. When this state of heart is arrived at, then is the third step in the discipline of one's self-seeking inclinations accomplished; then is the third great lesson in Virtue and Knowledge learned and mastered.

Having thus laid down the first ten steps and three lessons in right-doing and right-knowing, I leave those of my readers who are prepared for them to learn and master them in their everyday life. There is, of course, a still higher discipline of the body, a more far-reaching discipline of the tongue, and greater and more all-embracing virtues to acquire and understand before the highest state of bliss and knowledge can be apprehended, but it is not my purpose to deal with them here. I have expounded only the first and easiest lessons on the Higher Path, and by the time these are thoroughly mastered, the reader will have become so purified, strengthened, and enlightened, that he will not be left in the dark as to his future progress. Those of my readers who have completed these three lessons will already have perceived, beyond and above the high altitudes of Truth, and the narrow and precipitous track which leads to them, and will choose whether they shall proceed.

The straight Path which I have laid down can be pursued by all with greater profit to themselves and to the world, and even those who do not aspire to the attainment of Truth will develop greater intellectual and moral strength, finer judgment, and deeper peace of mind by perfecting themselves in this Path. Nor will their material prosperity suffer by this change of heart; nay, it will be rendered truer, purer, and more enduring, for if there is one who is capable of succeeding and fitted to achieve, it is the man who has abandoned the petty dissipations and everyday vices of his kind, who is strong to rule his body and his mind, and who pursues with fixed resolve the path of unswerving integrity and sterling virtue.

MENTAL CONDITIONS AND
THEIR EFFECTS

WITHOUT going into the details of the greater steps and lessons in the right life (a task outside the scope of this small work) a few hints and statements concerning those mental conditions from which life in its totality springs, will prove helpful to those who are ready and willing to penetrate further into that inner realm of heart and mind where Love and Wisdom and Peace await the strenuous comer.

All sin is ignorance. It is a condition of darkness and undevelopment. The wrong-thinker and wrong-doer is in the same position in the school of life as is the ignorant pupil in the school of learning. He has yet to learn how to think and act correctly, that is, in accordance with Law. The pupil in learning is not happy so long as he does his lessons wrongly, and unhappiness cannot be escaped while sin remains unconquered.

Life is a series of lessons. Some are diligent in learning them, and they become pure, wise, and altogether happy. Others are negligent, and do not apply themselves, and they remain impure, foolish, and unhappy.

Every form of unhappiness springs from a wrong condition of mind. Happiness inheres in right conditions of mind. Happiness is mental har-

mony; unhappiness is mental inharmony. While a man lives in wrong
conditions of mind, he will live a
wrong life, and will suffer continually.
Suffering is rooted in error. Bliss
inheres in enlightenment. There is
salvation for man only in the destruction of his own ignorance, error, and
self-delusion. Where there are wrong
conditions of mind there is bondage
and unrest; where there are right
conditions of mind there is freedom
and peace.

Here are some of the leading wrong
mental conditions and their disastrous
effects upon the life:

Wrong Mental Conditions	Their Effects
Hatred.	Injury, violence, disaster, and suffering.
Lust.	Confusion of intellect, re-

	morse, shame, and wretchedness.
Covetousness.	Fear, unrest, unhappiness, and loss.
Pride.	Disappointment, chagrin, lack of self-knowledge.
Vanity.	Distress, and mortification of spirit.
Condemnation.	Persecution, hatred from others.
Ill-will.	Failures and troubles.
Self-indulgence.	Misery, loss of judgment, grossness, disease, and neglect.
Anger.	Loss of power and influence.
Desire, or Self-Slavery.	Grief, folly, sorrow, uncertainty, and loneliness.

The above wrong conditions of mind are merely negations; they are states of darkness and deprivation and not of positive power. Evil is not a power; it is *ignorance and misuse of good.* The hater is he who has failed to do the lesson of Love correctly, and he suffers in consequence. When he succeeds in doing it rightly, the hatred will have disappeared, and he will see and understand the darkness and impotence of hatred. It is so with every wrong condition.

The following are some of the more important right mental conditions and their beneficent effects upon the life:

Right Mental Conditions.	Their Effects.
Love.	Gentle conditions, bliss, and blessedness.
Purity.	Intellectual clearness, joy, invincible confidence.
Selflessness.	Courage, satisfaction, happiness, and plenty.
Humility.	Calmness, restfulness, knowledge of Truth.
Meekness.	Equipoise, contentment under all circumstances.
Compassion.	Protection, love, and reverence from others.
Good-will.	Gladness and success.
Self-control.	Peace of mind, true judg-

	ment, refinement, health, and honour.
Patience.	Mental power, far-reaching influence.
Self-conquest.	Enlightenment, wisdom, insight, and profound peace.

The above right conditions of mind are states of positive power, of light, of joyful possession, and of knowledge. The good man *knows*. He has learned to do his lessons correctly, and thereby understands the exact proportions which make up the sum of life. He is enlightened, and knows good and evil. He is supremely happy, doing only that which is divinely right.

The man who is involved in the wrong conditions of mind, does not know. He is ignorant of good and evil, of himself, of the inward causes which make his life. He is unhappy,

and believes other people are entirely
the cause of his unhappiness. He
works blindly, and lives in darkness,
seeing no central purpose in existence,
and no orderly and lawful sequence
in the course of things.

He who aspires to the attainment
of the Higher Life in its completion
—who would perceive with unveiled
vision the true order of things and
the meaning of life—let him abandon
all the wrong conditions of heart, and
persevere unceasingly in the practice
of the good. If he suffers, or doubts,
or is unhappy, let him search within
until he finds the cause, and having
found it, let him cast it away. Let
him so guard and purify his heart
that every day less of evil and more
of good shall issue therefrom; so will
he daily become stronger, nobler, wiser;

so wiïl his blessedness increase, and the Light of Truth, growing ever brighter and brighter within him, will dispeï all gloom, and illuminate his Pathway.

EXHORTATION

DISCIPLES of Truth, lovers of Virtue, seekers of Wisdom; ye, also, who are sorrow stricken, knowing the emptiness of the self-life, and who aspire to the life that is supremely beautiful, and serenely glad,—take now yourselves in hand, enter the Door of Discipline, and know the Better Life.

Put away self-delusion; behold yourself as you are, and see the Path of Virtue as it is. There is no lazy way to Truth. He who would stand upon the mountain's summit must strenuously climb, and must rest only to gather strength. But if the climbing is less glorious than the cloudless summit, it is still glorious. Discipline in itself is beautiful, and the end of discipline is sweet.

Rise early and meditate. Begin each day with a conquered body, and a mind fortified against error and weakness. Temptation will never be overcome by unprepared fighting. The mind must be armed and arrayed in the silent hour. It must be trained to perceive, to know, to understand. Sin and temptation disappear when right understanding is developed.

Right understanding is reached through unabated discipline. Truth cannot be reached but through discipline. Patience will increase by effort and practice, and patience will make discipline beautiful.

Discipline is irksome to the impatient man and the self-lover, so he avoids it, and continues to live loosely and confusedly.

Discipline is not irksome to the Truth-lover, and he will find the infinite patience which can wait and work and overcome. As the joy of the gardener who sees his flowers develop day by day, so is the joy of the man of discipline who sees the divine flowers of Purity, Wisdom, Compassion, and Love, grow up in his heart.

The loose-liver cannot escape sorrow and pain. The undisciplined mind falls, weak and helpless, before the fierce onslaught of passion.

Array well your mind, then, lover of Truth. Be watchful, thoughtful resolute. Your salvation is at hand;

your readiness and effort are all that are needed. If you should fail ten times, do not be disheartened; if you should fail a hundred times, rise up and purpose your way; if you should fail a thousand times, do not despair. When the right Path is entered, success is sure if the Path is not utterly abandoned.

First strife, and then victory. First labour, and then rest. First weakness, and then strength. In the beginning the lower life, and the glare and confusion of battle, and at the end the Life Beautiful, the Silence, and the Peace.

THE END